SORROW AND DISMAY

SORROW AND DISMAY

ILLUSTRATED ANTI-WAR POEMS
OF CAPTAIN SIEGFRIED SASSOON

TCB Classics

Pompano Beach, Florida

TCB CLASSICS

An imprint of TCB Research & Indexing LLC
Pompano Beach, Florida

www.tcbinfosci.com/classic-books-with-indexes

ISBN 978-0-9996604-4-7 (hardcover)
ISBN 978-0-9996604-5-4 (ebook)
ISBN 978-0-9996604-6-1 (paperback)

Library of Congress Control Number: 2020941189

Printed in the United States of America

CONTENTS

ILLUSTRATIONS

FOREWORD

"My subject is War, and the pity of War. The poetry is in the pity."
—Wilfred Owen, Poets' Corner memorial, Westminster Abbey

The poet Siegfried Sassoon joined the British Army in 1914 full of patriotic fervor and a profound belief in a "just war." He volunteered willingly and was fearless on the battlefield. Yet his views changed radically during the Great War. Leading his men to slaughter, mutilation, and mental collapse wore him down. His heart broke. In July 1917, he wrote a letter of "willful defiance" disavowing the war. *(See a facsimile next to the poem "Banishment.")* He refused to return to duty. Instead of the expected court-martial, he was sent to a psychiatric war hospital where he was treated for shell shock—known as PTSD today. Eventually he did return to the Front.

Sassoon documented the horrors of war in poems riddled with blood and mud. The reader is confronted with dark details of tedium and battle. He often wrote with sarcasm on the motives of people in power and the absurdity of romantic views of war.

The vintage images complement his poems or offer wry counterpoint in sympathy with his views.

Siegfried Sassoon attained the rank of Captain and was decorated as a war hero. He is one of sixteen WWI poets commemorated in the Poets' Corner of Westminster Abbey.

—Tanja Bekhuis, PhD, Pompano Beach, Florida

DREAMERS

Soldiers are citizens of death's grey land,
　　　Drawing no dividend from time's tomorrows;
In the great hour of destiny they stand,
　　　Each with his feuds, and jealousies, and sorrows.
Soldiers are sworn to action; they must win
　　　Some flaming, fatal climax with their lives.
Soldiers are dreamers; when the guns begin
　　　They think of firelit homes, clean beds, and wives.

I see them in foul dugouts, gnawed by rats,
　　　And in the ruined trenches, lashed with rain,
Dreaming of things they did with balls and bats,
　　　And mocked by hopeless longing to regain
Bank holidays, and picture shows, and spats,
　　　And going to the office in the train.

2

TRENCH DUTY

Shaken from sleep, and numbed and scarce awake,
Out in the trench with three hours' watch to take,
I blunder through the splashing mirk; and then
Hear the gruff muttering voices of the men
Crouching in cabins candle-chinked with light.
Hark! There's the big bombardment on our right
Rumbling and bumping; and the dark's a glare
Of flickering horror in the sectors where
We raid the Boche; men waiting, stiff and chilled,
Or crawling on their bellies through the wire.
"What? Stretcher-bearers wanted? Some one killed?"
Five minutes ago I heard a sniper fire:
Why did he do it? — Starlight overhead —
Blank stars. I'm wide-awake; and some chap's dead.

WIRERS

"Pass it along, the wiring party's going out"—
And yawning sentries mumble, "Wirers going out."
Unravelling; twisting; hammering stakes with muffled
Thud, they toil with stealthy haste and
Anger in their blood.

The Boche sends up a flare. Black forms stand
Rigid there, stock-still like posts; then darkness, and the
Clumsy ghosts stride hither and thither, whispering,
tripped by clutching snare of snags and tangles.
Ghastly dawn with vaporous coasts
Gleams desolate along the sky, night's misery ended.

Young Hughes was badly hit; I heard him carried away,
Moaning at every lurch; no doubt he'll die today.
But we can say the frontline wire's been safely mended.

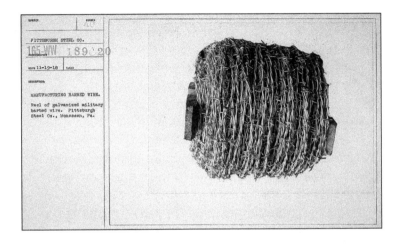

5

A WORKING PARTY

Three hours ago he blundered up the trench,
Sliding and poising, groping with his boots;
Sometimes he tripped and lurched against the walls
With hands that pawed the sodden bags of chalk.
He couldn't see the man who walked in front;
Only he heard the drum and rattle of feet
Stepping along the trenchboards—often splashing
Wretchedly where the sludge was ankle-deep.

Voices would grunt, "Keep to your right—make way!"
When squeezing past the men from the front line:
White faces peered, puffing a point of red;
Candles and braziers glinted through the chinks
And curtain flaps of dugouts; then the gloom
Swallowed his sense of sight; he stooped and swore
Because a sagging wire had caught his neck.
A flare went up; the shining whiteness spread
And flickered upward, showing nimble rats,
And mounds of glimmering sandbags,
Bleached with rain;
Then the slow, silver moment died in dark.

The wind came posting by with chilly gusts
And buffeting at corners, piping thin

And dreary through the crannies; rifle shots
Would split and crack and sing along the night,
And shells came calmly through the drizzling air
To burst with hollow bang below the hill.

Three hours ago he stumbled up the trench;
Now he will never walk that road again:
He must be carried back, a jolting lump
Beyond all need of tenderness and care;
A nine-stone corpse with nothing more to do.

He was a young man with a meagre wife
And two pale children in a Midland town;
He showed the photograph to all his mates;
And they considered him a decent chap
Who did his work and hadn't much to say,
And always laughed at other people's jokes
Because he hadn't any of his own.

That night, when he was busy at his job
Of piling bags along the parapet,
He thought how slow time went, stamping his feet,
And blowing on his fingers, pinched with cold.

He thought of getting back by half past twelve,
And tot of rum to send him warm to sleep,
In draughty dugout frowsty with the fumes
Of coke, and full of snoring, weary men.

He pushed another bag along the top,
Craning his body outward; then a flare
Gave one white glimpse of No Man's Land and wire;
And as he dropped his head the instant split
His startled life with lead, and all went out.

STAND-TO: GOOD FRIDAY MORNING

I'd been on duty from two till four.
I went and stared at the dugout door.
Down in the frowst I heard them snore.
"Stand-to!" Somebody grunted and swore.
    Dawn was misty; the skies were still;
    Larks were singing, discordant, shrill;
    They seemed happy; but *I* felt ill.
    Deep in water I splashed my way
Up the trench to our bogged front line.
Rain had fallen the whole damned night.
O Jesus, send me a wound today,
And I'll believe in Your bread and wine,
And get my bloody old sins washed white!

IN THE PINK

So Davies wrote: "This leaves me in the pink."
Then scrawled his name:
"Your loving sweetheart, Willie."
With crosses for a hug. He'd had a drink
Of rum and tea; and, though the barn was chilly,
For once his blood ran warm; he had pay to spend.
Winter was passing; soon the year would mend.

He couldn't sleep that night. Stiff in the dark
He groaned and thought of Sundays at the farm,
When he'd go out as cheerful as a lark
In his best suit to wander arm-in-arm
With brown-eyed Gwen, and whisper in her ear
The simple, silly things she liked to hear.

And then he thought: tomorrow night we trudge
Up to the trenches, and my boots are rotten.
Five miles of stodgy clay and freezing sludge,
And everything but wretchedness forgotten.
Tonight he's in the pink; but soon he'll die.
And still the war goes on; *he* don't know why.

IN AN UNDERGROUND
DRESSING STATION

Quietly they set their burden down: he tried to grin;
Moaned; moved his head from side to side.

———————

He gripped the stretcher; stiffened, glared, and
Screamed, "O put my leg down, doctor, do!"
(He'd got a bullet in his ankle; and he'd been shot
Horribly through the guts.)
The surgeon seemed so kind and gentle, saying,
Above that crying, "You must keep still, my lad."
But he was dying.

THE HAWTHORN TREE

Not much to me is yonder lane
   Where I go every day;
But when there's been a shower of rain
   And hedge birds whistle gay,
I know my lad that's out in France
   With fearsome things to see
Would give his eyes for just one glance
   At our white hawthorn tree.

———————

Not much to me is yonder lane
   Where *he* so longs to tread;
But when there's been a shower of rain
I think I'll never weep again
   Until I've heard he's dead.

14

SUICIDE IN TRENCHES

I knew a simple soldier boy
Who grinned at life in empty joy,
Slept soundly through the lonesome dark,
And whistled early with the lark.

In winter trenches, cowed and glum
With crumps and lice and lack of rum,
He put a bullet through his brain.
No one spoke of him again.

———————

You smug-faced crowds with kindling eye
Who cheer when soldier lads march by,
Sneak home and pray you'll never know
The hell where youth and laughter go.

THE HERO

"Jack fell as he'd have wished," the Mother said,
And folded up the letter that she'd read.
"The Colonel writes so nicely." Something broke
In the tired voice that quavered to a choke.
She half looked up. "We mothers are so proud
Of our dead soldiers." Then her face was bowed.

Quietly the Brother Officer went out.
He'd told the poor old dear some gallant lies
That she would nourish all her days, no doubt.
For while he coughed and mumbled, her weak eyes
Had shone with gentle triumph, brimmed with joy,
Because he'd been so brave, her glorious boy.

He thought how "Jack," cold-footed, useless swine,
Had panicked down the trench that night the mine
Went up at Wicked Corner; how he'd tried
To get sent home; and how, at last, he died,
Blown to small bits. And no one seemed to care
Except that lonely woman with white hair.

THE ROAD

The road is thronged with women; soldiers pass
And halt, but never see them; yet they're here—
A patient crowd along the sodden grass,
Silent, worn out with waiting, sick with fear.
The road goes crawling up a long hillside,
All ruts and stones and sludge, and the emptied dregs
Of battle thrown in heaps. Here where they died
Are stretched big-bellied horses with stiff legs;
And dead men, bloody-fingered from the fight,
Stare up at caverned darkness winking white.

You in the bomb-scorched kilt, poor sprawling Jock,
You tottered here and fell, and stumbled on,
Half dazed for want of sleep. No dream could mock
Your reeling brain with comforts lost and gone.
You did not feel her arms about your knees,
Her blind caress, her lips upon your head:
Too tired for thoughts of home and love and ease,
The road would serve you well enough for bed.

THE DREAM

Moonlight and dew-drenched blossom, and the scent
Of summer gardens; these can bring you all
Those dreams that in the starlit silence fall:
Sweet songs are full of odours.
                                    While I went
Last night in drizzling dusk along a lane,
I passed a squalid farm; from byre and midden
Came the rank smell that brought me once again
A dream of war that in the past was hidden.

                    II
Up a disconsolate straggling village street
I saw the tired troops trudge: I heard their feet.
The cheery QMS was there to meet
And guide our Company in ...
                                    I watched them stumble
Into some crazy hovel, too beat to grumble;
Saw them file inward, slipping from their backs
Rifles, equipment, packs.

On filthy straw they sit in the gloom, each face
Bowed to patched, sodden boots they must unlace,
While the wind chills their sweat through
Chinks and cracks.

III

I'm looking at their blistered feet; young Jones
Stares up at me, mud-splashed and white and jaded;
Out of his eyes the morning light has faded.
Old soldiers with three winters in their bones
Puff their damp Woodbines, whistle, stretch their toes
They can still grin at me, for each of 'em knows
That I'm as tired as they are ...
                              Can they guess
The secret burden that is always mine? —
Pride in their courage; pity for their distress;
And burning bitterness
That I must take them to the accursed Line.

IV

I cannot hear their voices, but I see
Dim candles in the barn: they gulp their tea,
And soon they'll sleep like logs. Ten miles away
The battle winks and thuds in blundering strife.
And I must lead them nearer, day by day,
To the foul beast of war that bludgeons life.

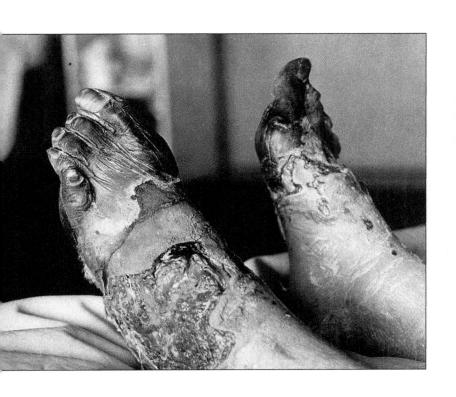

BATALLION RELIEF

"Fall in! Now, get a move on!" (Curse the rain.)
We splash away along the straggling village,
Out to the flat rich country green with June ...
And sunset flares across wet crops and tillage,
Blazing with splendour-patches. Harvest soon
Up in the Line. *"Perhaps the War'll be done
By Christmas time. Keep smiling then, old son!"*

Here's the Canal: it's dusk; we cross the bridge.
"Lead on there by platoons." The Line's aglare
With shellfire through the poplars; distant rattle
Of rifles and machine guns. *"Fritz is there!
Christ, ain't it lively, Sergeant? Is't a battle?"*
More rain: the lightning blinks, and thunder rumbles.
"There's overhead artillery," some chap grumbles.

"What's all this mob, by the crossroad?" (The guides) ...
"Lead on with Number One." (And off they go.)
"Three-minute intervals." ... Poor blundering files,
Sweating and blindly burdened; who's to know

If death will catch them in those two dark miles?
(More rain.) *"Lead on, Headquarters."* (That's the lot.)
"Who's that? O, Sergeant Major, don't get shot!
And tell me, have we won this war or not?"

THE REARGUARD

Groping along the tunnel, step by step,
He winked his prying torch with patching glare
From side to side, and sniffed the unwholesome air.

Tins, boxes, bottles, shapes too vague to know,
A mirror smashed, the mattress from a bed;
And he, exploring fifty feet below
The rosy gloom of battle overhead.

Tripping, he grabbed the wall; saw someone lie
Humped at his feet, half-hidden by a rug,
And stooped to give the sleeper's arm a tug.
"I'm looking for headquarters." No reply.
"God blast your neck!" (For days he'd had no sleep.)
"Get up and guide me through this stinking place."
Savage, he kicked a soft, unanswering heap,
And flashed his beam across the livid face
Terribly glaring up, whose eyes yet wore
Agony dying hard ten days before;
And fists of fingers clutched a blackening wound.

Alone he staggered on until he found
Dawn's ghost that filtered down a shafted stair
To the dazed, muttering creatures underground
Who hear the boom of shells in muffled sound.
At last, with sweat of horror in his hair,
He climbed through darkness to the twilight air,
Unloading hell behind him step by step.

HINDENBURG LINE,
APRIL 1917

I STOOD WITH THE DEAD

I stood with the Dead, so forsaken and still:
  When dawn was grey I stood with the Dead.
And my slow heart said, "You must kill, you must kill:
  Soldier, soldier, morning is red."

On the shapes of the slain in their crumpled disgrace
  I stared for a while through the thin cold rain …
"O lad that I loved, there is rain on your face,
  And your eyes are blurred and sick like the plain."

I stood with the Dead … They were dead; they were dead;
  My heart and my head beat a march of dismay:
And gusts of the wind came dulled by the guns …
  "Fall in!" I shouted; "Fall in for your pay!"

AT CARNOY

Down in the hollow there's the whole Brigade
Camped in four groups: through twilight falling slow
I hear a sound of mouth organs, ill-played,
And murmur of voices, gruff, confused, and low.
Crouched among thistle tufts I've watched the glow
Of a blurred orange sunset flare and fade;
And I'm content. Tomorrow we must go
To take some cursèd Wood ... O world God made!

ATTACK

At dawn the ridge emerges massed and dun
In the wild purple of the glowering sun
Smouldering through spouts of drifting smoke that shroud
The menacing scarred slope; and, one by one,
Tanks creep and topple forward to the wire.
The barrage roars and lifts. Then, clumsily bowed
With bombs and guns and shovels and battle gear,
Men jostle and climb to meet the bristling fire.
Lines of grey, muttering faces, masked with fear,
They leave their trenches, going over the top,
While time ticks blank and busy on their wrists,
And hope, with furtive eyes and grappling fists,
Flounders in mud. O Jesus, make it stop!

COUNTERATTACK

We'd gained our first objective hours before
While dawn broke like a face with blinking eyes,
Pallid, unshaved and thirsty, blind with smoke.
Things seemed all right at first. We held their line,
With bombers posted, Lewis guns well placed,
And clink of shovels deepening the shallow trench.
The place was rotten with dead; green clumsy legs
High-booted, sprawled and grovelled along the saps
And trunks, face downward in the sucking mud,
Wallowed like trodden sandbags loosely filled;
And naked sodden buttocks, mats of hair,
Bulged, clotted heads, slept in the plastering slime.
And then the rain began—the jolly old rain!

A yawning soldier knelt against the bank,
Staring across the morning blear with fog;
He wondered when the Allemands would get busy;
And then, of course, they start'd with five-nines
Traversing, sure as fate, and never a dud.
Mute in the clamour of shells he watched them burst
Spouting dark earth and wire with gusts from hell,
While posturing giants dissolved in drifts of smoke.
He crouched and flinched, dizzy with galloping fear,

Sick for escape—loathing the strangled horror
And butchered, frantic gestures of the dead.

An officer came blundering down the trench:
"Stand-to and man the fire step!" On he went ...
Gasping and bawling, "Fire step ... counterattack!"
Then the haze lifted. Bombing on the right
Down the old sap: machine guns on the left;
And stumbling figures looming out in front.
"O Christ, they're coming at us!" Bullets spat,
And he remembered his rifle ... rapid fire ...
And started blazing wildly ... then a bang
Crumpled and spun him sideways, knocked him out
To grunt and wriggle: none heeded him; he choked
And fought the flapping veils of smothering gloom,
Lost in a blurred confusion of yells and groans.
Down, and down, and down, he sank and drowned,
Bleeding to death. The counterattack had failed.

THE EFFECT

"The effect of our bombardment was terrific.
One man told me he had never seen so many dead before."
— War correspondent

"He'd never seen so many dead before."
They sprawled in yellow daylight while he swore
And gasped and lugged his everlasting load
Of bombs along what once had been a road.
"How peaceful are the dead."
Who put that silly gag in someone's head?

"He'd never seen so many dead before."
The lilting words danced up and down his brain,
While corpses jumped and capered in the rain.
No, no, he wouldn't count them anymore ...
The dead have done with pain:
They've choked; they can't come back to life again.

When Dick was killed last week he looked like that,
Flapping along the fire step like a fish,
After the blazing crump had knocked him flat ...
"How many dead? As many as ever you wish.
Don't count 'em; they're too many.
Who'll buy my nice fresh corpses, two a penny?"

REMORSE

Lost in the swamp and welter of the pit,
He flounders off the duckboards; only he knows
Each flash and spouting crash—each instant lit
When gloom reveals the streaming rain. He goes
Heavily, blindly on. And, while he blunders,
"Could anything be worse than this?"—he wonders,
Remembering how he saw those Germans run,
Screaming for mercy among the stumps of trees:
Green-faced, they dodged and darted: there was one
Livid with terror, clutching at his knees ...
Our chaps were sticking 'em like pigs ... "O hell !"
He thought "there's things in war one dare not tell
Poor father sitting safe at home, who reads
Of dying heroes and their deathless deeds."

DIED OF WOUNDS

His wet, white face and miserable eyes
Brought nurses to him more than groans and sighs:
But hoarse and low and rapid rose and fell
His troubled voice: he did the business well.

The ward grew dark; but he was still complaining,
And calling out for "Dickie." "Curse the Wood!
It's time to go; O Christ, and what's the good? —
We'll never take it; and it's always raining."

I wondered where he'd been; then heard him shout,
"They snipe like hell! O Dickie, don't go out" ...
I fell asleep ... next morning he was dead;
And some Slight Wound lay smiling on his bed.

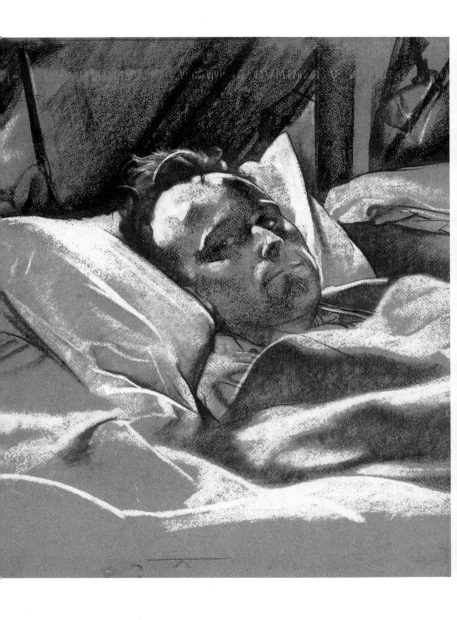

LAMENTATIONS

I found him in a guardroom at the Base.
From the blind darkness I had heard his crying
And blundered in. With puzzled, patient face
A sergeant watched him; it was no good trying
To stop it; for he howled and beat his chest.
And, all because his brother had gone West,
Raved at the bleeding war; his rampant grief
Moaned, shouted, sobbed, and choked, while he was kneeling
Half-naked on the floor. In my belief
Such men have lost all patriotic feeling.

HOW TO DIE

Dark clouds are smouldering into red
    While down the craters morning burns.
The dying soldier shifts his head
    To watch the glory that returns:
He lifts his fingers toward the skies
    Where holy brightness breaks in flame;
Radiance reflected in his eyes,
    And on his lips a whispered name.

You'd think, to hear some people talk,
    That lads go West with sobs and curses,
And sullen faces white as chalk,
    Hankering for wreaths and tombs and hearses.
But they've been taught the way to do it
    Like Christian soldiers; not with haste
And shuddering groans; but passing through it
    With due regard for decent taste.

FIGHT TO A FINISH

The boys came back. Bands played and flags were flying,
    And Yellow Pressmen thronged the sunlit street
To cheer the soldiers who'd refrained from dying,
    And hear the music of returning feet.
"Of all the thrills and ardours War has brought,
This moment is the finest." (So they thought.)

Snapping their bayonets on to charge the mob,
    Grim Fusiliers broke ranks with glint of steel.
At last the boys had found a cushy job.

———————

I heard the Yellow Pressmen grunt and squeal;
And with my trusty bombers turned and went
To clear those Junkers out of Parliament.

ATROCITIES

You told me, in your drunken-boasting mood,
How once you butchered prisoners. That was good!
I'm sure you felt no pity while they stood
Patient and cowed and scared, as prisoners should.

How did you do them in? Come, don't be shy:
You know I love to hear how Germans die,
Downstairs in dugouts. "Camerad!" they cry;
Then squeal like stoats when bombs begin to fly.

———————

And you? I know your record. You went sick
When orders looked unwholesome: then, with trick
And lie, you wangled home. And here you are,
Still talking big and boozing in a bar.

WHEN I'M AMONG A BLAZE OF LIGHTS ...

When I'm among a blaze of lights,
With tawdry music and cigars
And women dawdling through delights,
And officers at cocktail bars—
Sometimes I think of garden nights
And elm trees nodding at the stars.

I dream of a small firelit room
With yellow candles burning straight,
And glowing pictures in the gloom,
And kindly books that hold me late.
Of things like these I love to think
When I can never be alone:
Then someone says, "Another drink?"—
And turns my living heart to stone.

GLORY OF WOMEN

You love us when we're heroes, home on leave,
Or wounded in a mentionable place.
You worship decorations; you believe
That chivalry redeems the war's disgrace.
You make us shells. You listen with delight,
By tales of dirt and danger fondly thrilled.
You crown our distant ardours while we fight,
And mourn our laurelled memories when we're killed.

You can't believe that British troops "retire"
When hell's last horror breaks them, and they run,
Trampling the terrible corpses—blind with blood.
O German mother dreaming by the fire,
While you are knitting socks to send your son
His face is trodden deeper in the mud.

THEIR FRAILTY

He's got a Blighty wound. He's safe; and then
    War's fine and bold and bright.
She can forget the doomed and prisoned men
    Who agonize and fight.

He's back in France. She loathes the listless strain
    And peril of his plight.
Beseeching Heaven to send him home again,
    She prays for peace each night.

Husbands and sons and lovers; everywhere
    They die; War bleeds us white.
Mothers and wives and sweethearts—they don't care
    So long as He's all right.

DOES IT MATTER?

Does it matter? — losing your legs? ...
For people will always be kind,
And you need not show that you mind
When the others come in after football
To gobble their muffins and eggs.

Does it matter? — losing your sight? ...
There's such splendid work for the blind;
And people will always be kind,
As you sit on the terrace remembering
And turning your face to the light.

Do they matter? — those dreams from the pit? ...
You can drink and forget and be glad,
And people won't say that you're mad;
For they'll know that you've fought for your country,
And no one will worry a bit.

BANISHMENT

I am banished from the patient men who fight.
They smote my heart to pity, built my pride.
Shoulder to aching shoulder, side by side,
They trudged away from life's broad wealds of light.
Their wrongs were mine; and ever in my sight
They went arrayed in honour. But they died—
Not one by one: and mutinous I cried
To those who sent them out into the night.

The darkness tells how vainly I have striven
To free them from the pit where they must dwell
In outcast gloom convulsed and jagged and riven
By grappling guns. Love drove me to rebel.
Love drives me back to grope with them through hell;
And in their tortured eyes I stand forgiven.

by

.o. Lt. Siegfried Sassoon.

3rd Batt: Royal Welsh Fusiliers.

July, 1917.

I am making this statement as an act of wilful defiance of
military authority because I believe that the war is being deliberately
prolonged by those who have the power to end it. I am a soldier, con-
vinced that I am acting on behalf of soldiers. I believe that the war
upon which I entered as a war of defence and liberation has now become
a war of aggression and conquest. I believe that the purposes for which
I and my fellow soldiers entered upon this war should have been so
clearly stated as to have made it impossible to change them and that had
this been done the objects which actuated us would now be attainable by
negotiation.

I have seen and endured the sufferings of the troops and I
can no longer be a party to prolong these sufferings for ends which I
believe to be evil and unjust. I am not protesting against the conduct
of the war, but against the political errors and insincerities for which
the fighting men are being sacrificed.

On behalf of those who are suffering now, I make this protest
against the deception which is being practised upon them; also I believe
it may help to destroy the callous complacency with which the majority
of those at home regard the continuance of agonies which they do not
share and which they have not enough imagination to realise.

SURVIVORS

No doubt they'll soon get well; the shock and strain
Have caused their stammering, disconnected talk.
Of course they're "longing to go out again"—
These boys with old, scared faces, learning to walk,
They'll soon forget their haunted nights; their cowed
Subjection to the ghosts of friends who died—
Their dreams that drip with murder; and they'll be proud
Of glorious war that shatter'd all their pride …
Men who went out to battle, grim and glad;
Children, with eyes that hate you, broken and mad.

CRAIGLOCKHART, OCTOBER 1917

ARMS AND THE MAN

Young Croesus went to pay his call
On Colonel Sawbones, Caxton Hall:
And, though his wound was healed and mended,
He hoped he'd get his leave extended.

The waiting room was dark and bare.
He eyed a neat-framed notice there
Above the fireplace hung to show
Disabled heroes where to go
For arms and legs; with scale of price,
And words of dignified advice
How officers could get them free.

Elbow or shoulder, hip or knee—
Two arms, two legs, though all were lost,
They'd be restored him free of cost.

Then a Girl Guide looked in to say,
"Will Captain Croesus come this way?"

TO ANY DEAD OFFICER

Well, how are things in Heaven? I wish you'd say,
  Because I'd like to know that you're all right.
Tell me, have you found everlasting day,
  Or been sucked in by everlasting night?
For when I shut my eyes your face shows plain;
  I hear you make some cheery old remark—
I can rebuild you in my brain,
  Though you've gone out patrolling in the dark.

You hated tours of trenches; you were proud
  Of nothing more than having good years to spend;
Longed to get home and join the careless crowd
  Of chaps who work in peace with Time for friend.
That's all washed out now. You're beyond the wire;
  No earthly chance can send you crawling back;
You've finished with machine-gun fire—
  Knocked over in a hopeless dud attack.

Somehow I always thought you'd get done in,
  Because you were so desperate keen to live:
You were all out to try and save your skin,
  Well knowing how much the world had got to give.
You joked at shells and talked the usual "shop,"
  Stuck to your dirty job and did it fine:
With "Jesus Christ! when *will* it stop?
  Three years ... It's hell unless we break their line."

So when they told me you'd been left for dead
 I wouldn't believe them, feeling it *must* be true.
Next week the bloody Roll of Honour said
 "Wounded and missing"— (That's the thing to do
When lads are left in shell holes dying slow,
 With nothing but blank sky and wounds that ache,
Moaning for water till they know
 It's night, and then it's not worth while to wake!)

———————

Goodbye, old lad! Remember me to God.
 And tell Him that our Politicians swear
They won't give in till Prussian Rule's been trod
 Under the Heel of England … Are you there? …
Yes … and the War won't end for at least two years;
But we've got stacks of men … I'm blind with tears,
 Staring into the dark. Cheero!
I wish they'd killed you in a decent show.

THE ONE-LEGGED MAN

Propped on a stick he viewed the August weald;
Squat orchard trees and oasts with painted cowls;
A homely, tangled hedge, a corn-stooked field,
With sound of barking dogs and farmyard fowls.

And he'd come home again to find it more
Desirable than ever it was before.
How right it seemed that he should reach the span
Of comfortable years allowed to man!

Splendid to eat and sleep and choose a wife,
Safe with his wound, a citizen of life.
He hobbled blithely through the garden gate,
And thought: "Thank God they had to amputate!"

SICK LEAVE

When I'm asleep, dreaming and lulled and warm—
They come, the homeless ones, the noiseless dead.
While the dim charging breakers of the storm
Bellow and drone and rumble overhead,
Out of the gloom they gather about my bed.
They whisper to my heart; their thoughts are mine.
"Why are you here with all your watches ended?
From Ypres to Frise we sought you in the Line."
In bitter safety I awake, unfriended;
And while the dawn begins with slashing rain
I think of the Battalion in the mud.
"When are you going out to them again?
Are they not still your brothers through our blood?"

REPRESSION OF WAR EXPERIENCE

Now light the candles; one, two, there's a moth;
What silly beggars they are to blunder in
And scorch their wings with glory, liquid flame—
No, no, not that—it's bad to think of war,
When thoughts you've gagged all day come back to
Scare you;
And it's been proved that soldiers don't go mad
Unless they lose control of ugly thoughts
That drive them out to jabber among the trees.

Now light your pipe; look, what a steady hand.
Draw a deep breath; stop thinking; count fifteen,
And you're as right as rain ...
                              Why won't it rain? ...
I wish there'd be a thunderstorm tonight,
With bucketsful of water to sluice the dark,
And make the roses hang their dripping heads.

Books, what a jolly company they are,
Standing so quiet and patient on their shelves,
Dressed in dim brown, and black, and white, and green
And every kind of colour. Which will you read?
Come on; O *do* read something; they're so wise.
I tell you all the wisdom of the world

Is waiting for you on those shelves; and yet
You sit and gnaw your nails, and let your pipe out,
And listen to the silence: on the ceiling
There's one big, dizzy moth that bumps and flutters;
And in the breathless air outside the house
The garden waits for something that delays.
There must be crowds of ghosts among the trees—
Not people killed in battle—they're in France—
But horrible shapes in shrouds—old men who died
Slow, natural deaths—old men with ugly souls,
Who wore their bodies out with nasty sins.

———————

You're quiet and peaceful, summering safe at home;
You'd never think there was a bloody war on! ...
O yes, you would ... why, you can hear the guns.
Hark! Thud, thud, thud—quite soft ... they never cease—
Those whispering guns—O Christ, I want to go out
And screech at them to stop—I'm going crazy;
I'm going stark, staring mad because of the guns.

NIGHT ON THE CONVOY

ALEXANDRIA-MARSEILLES

Out in the blustering darkness, on the deck
A gleam of stars looks down. Long blurs of black,
The lean Destroyers, level with our track,
Plunging and stealing, watch the perilous way
Through backward racing seas and caverns of chill spray.

One sentry by the davits, in the gloom
Stands mute; the boat heaves onward through the night.
Shrouded is every chink of cabined light:
And sluiced by floundering waves that hiss and boom
And crash like guns, the troopship shudders ... doom.

Now something at my feet stirs with a sigh;
And slowly growing used to groping dark,
I know that the hurricane deck, down all its length,
Is heaped and spread with lads in sprawling strength—

Blanketed soldiers sleeping. In the stark
Danger of life at war, they lie so still,
All prostrate and defenceless, head by head ...
And I remember Arras, and that hill
Where dumb with pain I stumbled among the dead.

———————

We are going home. The troopship, in a thrill
Of fiery-chamber'd anguish, throbs and rolls.
We are going home—victims—three thousand souls.

MAY 1918

RECONCILIATION

When you are standing at your hero's grave,
Or near some homeless village where he died,
Remember, through your heart's rekindling pride,
The German soldiers who were loyal and brave.

Men fought like brutes; and hideous things were done:
And you have nourished hatred, harsh and blind.
But in that Golgotha perhaps you'll find
The mothers of the men who killed your son.

NOVEMBER 1918

"THEY"

The Bishop tells us: "When the boys come back
They will not be the same; for they'll have fought
In a just cause: they lead the last attack
On Anti-Christ; their comrade's blood has bought
New right to breed an honourable race.
They have challenged Death and dared him face to face."

"We're none of us the same!" the boys reply.
"For George lost both his legs; and Bill's stone blind;
Poor Jim's shot through the lungs and like to die;
And Bert's gone syphilitic: you'll not find
A chap who's served that hasn't found *some* change."
And the Bishop said: "The ways of God are strange!"

BASE DETAILS

If I were fierce, and bald, and short of breath,
    I'd live with scarlet Majors at the Base,
And speed glum heroes up the line to death.
    You'd see me with my puffy petulant face,
Guzzling and gulping in the best hotel,
    Reading the Roll of Honour. "Poor young chap,"
I'd say—"I used to know his father well;
    Yes, we've lost heavily in this last scrap."
And when the war is done and youth stone dead,
I'd toddle safely home and die—in bed.

EDITOR   CAPITALIST   POLITICIAN   MINISTER

The Masses

MEMORIAL TABLET

GREAT WAR

Squire nagged and bullied till I went to fight
(Under Lord Derby's scheme). I died in hell—
(They called it Passchendaele); my wound was slight,
And I was hobbling back, and then a shell
Burst slick upon the duckboards; so I fell
Into the bottomless mud, and lost the light.

In sermon-time, while Squire is in his pew,
He gives my gilded name a thoughtful stare;
For though low down upon the list, I'm there:
"In proud and glorious memory"—that's my due.
Two bleeding years I fought in France for Squire;
I suffered anguish that he's never guessed;
Once I came home on leave; and then went West.
What greater glory could a man desire?

THE DEATHBED

He drowsed and was aware of silence heaped
Round him, unshaken as the steadfast walls;
Aqueous like floating rays of amber light,
Soaring and quivering in the wings of sleep—
Silence and safety; and his mortal shore
Lipped by the inward, moonless waves of death.

Someone was holding water to his mouth.
He swallowed, unresisting; moaned and dropped
Through crimson gloom to darkness; and forgot
The opiate throb and ache that was his wound.
Water—calm, sliding green above the weir;
Water—a skylit alley for his boat,
Bird-voiced, and bordered with reflected flowers
And shaken hues of summer: drifting down,
He dipped contented oars, and sighed, and slept.

Night, with a gust of wind, was in the ward,
Blowing the curtain to a glimmering curve.
Night. He was blind; he could not see the stars
Glinting among the wraiths of wandering cloud;
Queer blots of colour, purple, scarlet, green,
Flickered and faded in his drowning eyes.

Rain—he could hear it rustling through the dark;
Fragrance and passionless music woven as one;
Warm rain on drooping roses; pattering showers
That soak the woods; not the harsh rain that sweeps
Behind the thunder, but a trickling peace
Gently and slowly washing life away.

He stirred, shifting his body; then the pain
Leaped like a prowling beast, and gripped and tore
His groping dreams with grinding claws and fangs.
But someone was beside him; soon he lay
Shuddering because that evil thing had passed.
And Death, who'd stepped toward him, paused and stared.

Light many lamps and gather round his bed.
Lend him your eyes, warm blood, and will to live.
Speak to him; rouse him; you may save him yet.
He's young; he hated war; how should he die
When cruel old campaigners win safe through?

But Death replied: "I choose him." So he went,
And there was silence in the summer night;
Silence and safety; and the veils of sleep.
Then, far away, the thudding of the guns.

AFTERMATH

Have you forgotten yet? ...
For the world's events have rumbled on since those
Gagged days, like traffic checked awhile at the
Crossing of city ways:
And the haunted gap in your mind has filled with
Thoughts that flow like clouds in the lit heavens of life;
And you're a man reprieved to go, taking your peaceful
Share of Time, with joy to spare.
But the past is just the same—and War's a bloody game ...
Have you forgotten yet? ...
Look down, and swear by the slain of the War that
You'll Never forget.

Do you remember the dark months you held
The sector at Mametz—
The nights you watched and wired and dug and piled
Sandbags on parapets?
Do you remember the rats; and the stench of
Corpses rotting in front of the front-line trench—
And dawn coming, dirty white, and chill with a
Hopeless rain? Do you ever stop and ask,
"Is it all going to happen again?"

Do you remember that hour of din before the attack—
And the anger, the blind compassion that seized and
Shook you then as you peered at the doomed and
Haggard faces of your men?

Do you remember the stretcher-cases lurching
Back with dying eyes and lolling heads—
Those ashen-grey masks of the lads who once
Were keen and kind and gay?

Have you forgotten yet? ...
Look up, and swear by the green of the Spring that
You'll never forget.

Do you remember the stretcher-cases lurching
Back with dying eyes and lolling heads—
Those ashen-grey masks of the lads who once
Were keen and kind and gay?

Have you forgotten yet? ...
Look up, and swear by the green of the Spring that
You'll never forget.

TWO HUNDRED YEARS AFTER

Trudging by Corbie Ridge one winter's night,
(Unless old, hearsay memories tricked his sight),
Along the pallid edge of the quiet sky
He watched a nosing lorry grinding on,
And straggling files of men; when these were gone,
A double limber and six mules went by,
Hauling the rations up through ruts and mud
To trenchlines digged two hundred years ago.
Then darkness hid them with a rainy scud,
And soon he saw the village lights below.

But when he'd told his tale, an old man said
That *he'd* seen soldiers pass along that hill;
"Poor, silent things, they were the English dead
Who came to fight in France and got their fill."

INDEX OF FIRST LINES

L

Lost in the swamp and welter of the pit 33

M

Moonlight and dew-drenched blossom, and the scent 18

N

No doubt they'll soon get well; the shock and strain 50
Not much to me is yonder lane 13
Now light the candles; one, two, there's a moth 56

O

Out in the blustering darkness, on the deck 58

P

"Pass it along, the wiring party's going out" 4
Propped on a stick he viewed the August weald 54

Q

Quietly they set their burden down: he tried 11

S

Shaken from sleep, and numbed and scarce awake 3
So Davies wrote: "This leaves me in the pink." 10
Soldiers are citizens of death's grey land 1
Squire nagged and bullied till I went to fight 65

T
The Bishop tells us: "When the boys come back 62
The boys came back. Bands played and flags were flying 38
"The effect of our bombardment was terrific. 32
The road is thronged with women; soldiers pass 17
Three hours ago he blundered up the trench 6
Trudging by Corbie Ridge one winter's night 71

W
We'd gained our first objective hours before 30
Well, how are things in Heaven? I wish you'd say 52
When I'm among a blaze of lights 41
When I'm asleep, dreaming and lulled and warm 55
When you are standing at your hero's grave 60

Y
You love us when we're heroes, home on leave 43
Young Croesus went to pay his call 51
You told me, in your drunken-boasting mood 39

CREDITS

Cover   Bad news—A má notícia (Belmiro de Almeida, painting, 1897). Museu Mineiro, Belo Horizonte, Brazil. https://commons. wikimedia.org/wiki/File:Belmiro_de_Almeida_-_A_m%C3%A1_ not%C3%ADcia.jpg

Frontispiece   Mourning iris (Anselmus Boëtius de Bood, illustration, 1596–1610). Rijksmuseum, Amsterdam. https://www.rijksmuseum.nl/nl/collectie/RP-T-BR-2017-1-9-104

x   Australian infantry with small box respirators in Ypres (James Francis Hurley, photo, 1917). Australian War Memorial, Campbell. https://www.awm.gov.au/collection/E00825

2   Orderlies caring for wounded in a trench (anon., painting, n.d.). Wellcome Library, London. https://wellcomecollection.org/works/ xgn4zwqe

5   Military barbed wire (Pittsburgh Steel, photo, 1917–1918). US National Archives and Records Administration, College Park, MD. https://catalog.archives.gov/id/31486017

8   Two young girls (Gertrude Jekyll, photo, 1908). *Children and Gardens* by Gertrude Jekyll (Country Life Library, 1908). https://commons.wikimedia.org/wiki/File:Children_and_gardens_ (1908)_(14592167788).jpg. Comment: Photo from a scanned book in the Internet Archive.

11   Underground dressing station (anon., unknown medium, n.d.). Wellcome Library, London. https://wellcomecollection.org/works/ qxvacjv6

12   White hawthorn (Sten Porse, photo, 2007). Wikimedia Commons. https://commons.wikimedia.org/wiki/File: Crataegus-oxyacantha-flowers.JPG

14   Sacrificial lamb (Josefa de Óbidos, painting, c. 1670– c. 1684). The Walters Art Museum, Baltimore. https://art.thewalters.org/detail/8783/the-sacrificial-lamb/

20   Where Tommy's footwear is repaired (John Warwick Brooke, photo, 1916–1918). National Library of Scotland, Edinburgh. https://www.flickr.com/photos/nlscotland/2957907639/. Comment: 30,000 pairs of boots were repaired each week in this shop.

21   Trench feet (Albert Norman RAMC, photo, n.d.). Wellcome Library, London. https://commons.wikimedia.org/wiki/File:Trench_feet._Wellcome_L0025834.jpg.

27   "Fall In" (anon., poster, c. 1915). Library of Congress Prints and Photographs Division, Washington, DC. http://loc.gov/pictures/resource/cph.3g10987/. Comment: British recruitment poster.

28   Thistles (Alexey Klen, photo, 2009). Pixabay. https://pixabay.com/photos/nature-plant-thorn-flower-thistle-3145271/

33   Soldiers on a duckboard near Ypres (James Francis Hurley, photo, 1917). Australian War Memorial, Campbell. https://www.awm.gov.au/collection/E01220

35   Wounded man in a hospital bed (Eric Henri Kennington, pastel, n.d.). Imperial War Museum. https://www.iwm.org.uk/collections/item/object/15132

40   Man reading (John Singer Sargent, painting, 1904–1908). Reading Public Museum, Reading, PA. https://commons.wikimedia.org/wiki/File:%27Man_Reading%27_by_John_Singer_Sargent,_Reading_Public_Museum.jpg

42   Women in shell factory (Bain News Service, photo, c. 1915). Library of Congress, Washington, DC. https://www.loc.gov/pictures/item/2014706010/

44   Wounded soldier welcomed home (*Sydney Mail*, 1918). Australian War Memorial, Campbell. https://www.awm.gov.au/collection/C322766

47   The scream (Edvard Munch, painting, 1893). National Gallery of Norway, Oslo. https://www.nasjonalmuseet.no/samlingen/objekt/NG.M.00939

49   Sassoon's letter of protest (Siegfried Sassoon, letter, 1917). Wikisource. https://en.wikisource.org/wiki/File:Sasssoon-against-war-letter.jpg

59   Sunset at sea (Thomas Moran, painting, c. 1906). Brooklyn Museum. https://www.brooklynmuseum.org/opencollection/objects/415

61   Women of Britain say "Go!" (E. J. Kealey, poster, 1915). Te Papa Tongarewa (The Museum of New Zealand), Wellington. https://collections.tepapa.govt.nz/object/958810

64   Having their fling (Arthur Henry Young, anti-war cartoon, 1917). *The Masses*. http://dlib.nyu.edu/themasses/books/masses077/#7

69   Hope (George Frederic Watts and assistants, painting, 1886). Tate Britain, London. https://commons.wikimedia.org/wiki/File:Assistants_and_George_Frederic_Watts_-_Hope_-_Google_Art_Project.jpg

70   Middlesex [Regiment] returning from the trenches in the pouring rain (Ernest Brooks, photo, 1916 to 1918). National Library of Scotland, Edinburgh. https://digital.nls.uk/74545968

CPSIA information can be obtained
at www.ICGtesting.com
Printed in the USA
BVHW020720100122
625865BV00019B/469